BRAINY BREAKFASTS

Brainy Breakfasts: Over 40 Grain-Free, Brain-Boosting Breakfasts for Kids and Their Parents

Copyright © Trisha Gilkerson | IntoxicatedOnLife.com

ISBN-13: 978-1530162543

ISBN-10: 1530162548

Cover photo by Renee Kohley from RaisingGenerationNourished.com

Publishing and Design Serves | MelindaMartin.me

BRAINY BREAKFASTS

Over 40 Grain-Free, Brain-Fueling Breakfasts for Kids & Their Parents

BRAINY BREAKFASTS

Eggs

"Cereals"

Baked Goods

Waffles, Donuts, and Pancakes

Smoothies

Other Fun Breakfast Options

Contributing Authors

Trisha Gilkerson | IntoxicatedOnLife.com

Raia Todd | RaiasRecipes.com

Kelli Becton | AdventureHomeschool.com and FrugalMommas.com

Sarah Robinson | SidetrackedSarah.com

Jessica Young | SimplyHealthyHome.com

Amanda Espinoza | CountingAllJoy.com

TJ Sugden | MeasuringFlower.com

Jennifer Saleem | HybridRastaMama.com

Lynnae McCoy | LynnaeMcCoy.com

Chantelle Marie Swayne | HappyHealthyHolyHome.com

Renee Kohley | RaisingGenerationNourished.com

Paula Miller | WholeIntentions.com

Sammi Ricke | GroundedAndSurrounded.com

Becky Marie | ForThisSeason.com

Introduction

What does breakfast look like at your house? I'm going to be honest. In my house, it can sometimes be a less-than-ideal environment.

Our kids get tired of eating the normal healthy breakfasts we put in front of them. They want to know why they can't eat the brightly colored, sugar-filled cereals, Pop-Tarts®, and other convenience foods they see.

Quite frankly, sometimes it feels like it would be nice to throw those convenience foods at them. It certainly would be a lot easier. But I also know both the short and long-term implications of feeding them processed, sugar-filled foods.

Not to mention, because I homeschool my children, if I don't feed my kids a good breakfast, I am the one who has to deal with the fallout—the moodiness and the hunger pangs that come just an hour after breakfast.

Just the other day, my son wasn't too thrilled with the breakfast options I gave him, so he went without. He just said he wasn't hungry and walked away. The rest of the morning was worthless. School work? What's that? He was distracted by his hungry belly and his mind wouldn't stay focused.

The fact that I consistently struggle with delicious, healthy breakfast options for my family made me suspect that other parents do too. I certainly can't be the only mother out there with this problem. That was the inspiration for this book.

I was delighted to partner with a number of other highly talented authors to create a cookbook filled with over 40 delicious breakfasts. The vision behind *Brainy Breakfasts* was to provide myself (and you, the reader) with a handy guide to making breakfasts that build the brain, getting your kids (and you) mentally ready for the day ahead.

What Does the Research Say About Breakfast?

In our family, trying new recipes adds more excitement and interest to the meals. If you know me, in addition to experimenting in the kitchen, you know I enjoy reading peer reviewed research journals—for fun. When I was working on my master's degree, I was on the research team—for fun.

Ok, maybe I'm a little bit of a geek. But hopefully you'll still like me.

The research says breakfast is an important meal, especially for our kids who have developing brains. The literature on what types of foods are most important really isn't all that complex. This topic can be summed up quite concisely:

- Breakfast-eaters consistently academically out-perform non-breakfast-eaters.

- High-carb breakfast content negatively impacts test scores.

- Lack of protein in breakfast correlates with low school performance.

- The most important components of a breakfast that supports brain function and neurotransmitter activity include: protein, fat, B vitamins, iron, choline, and antioxidants.

How do high-sugar, highly-processed breakfasts impact our kids?

And what about those brightly colored, sugary cereals that just call our children's names and tempt us to give in? How do those processed foods impact our kids in the morning?

- A high-carb meal with lots of sugar will lead to a sugar crash. Our kids will end up hungry, distracted, probably temperamental, and they won't perform well while doing school work.

- A meal without plenty of healthy fats starves the brain. Did you know your brain is primarily made up of fat (mostly saturated fat) and cholesterol?

- Meals made up of primarily processed foods can set your child up for a lifetime of bad eating habits that lead to disease. It's so much easier to instill good eating habits in them while they're young!

The Brainy Ingredients

Breakfasts that give your brain great fuel must start with high-quality ingredients. I'd like to highlight a number of the ingredients that are the particularly important, brain-fueling ingredients found throughout this cookbook.

Eggs

Eggs. One of the healthiest foods for your morning.

Eggs have long been touted by food scientists as one of the healthiest foods you can eat. All the while, the USDA has vilified the egg as being too cholesterol-laden.

Finally, the USDA has begun to catch up with modern science and is revising their dietary guidelines. In the past they have recommended no more than 300 mg of dietary cholesterol, but in their recent guidelines they state, "Cholesterol is not a nutrient of concern for overconsumption."

You see, the USDA has finally been adequately convinced by the mounting evidence that *it isn't dietary cholesterol that raises blood cholesterol levels*. I'm not sure they realize that it's inflammation and inflammation-causing foods that raise cholesterol levels...but it's a start in the right direction.

Eggs are packed with essential fatty acids and are rich in protein. This qualifies eggs as one of the best foods you can eat to start your morning.

Egg yolks are among the richest and easiest natural sources of choline, providing 26.5% of the daily value in a single large egg. Choline is a B-complex vitamin that is an important building block of brain cells. It works by stimulating the production of a key neurotransmitter: Acetycholine. This neurotransmitter is responsible for memory, mental clarity and focus, and the healthy formation of synaptic connections between neurons.

If that isn't enough to make you consider frequently adding eggs to your morning menu, consider the following about eggs:

- Eggs are one of the only foods that contain naturally occurring vitamin D.

- Eggs encourage hair and nail growth because of their high sulfur content.

- Eggs contain antioxidants that help protect your eyes.

- Eggs contain numerous other important vitamins and minerals.

Coconut

Whether we're talking about coconut flour, oil, flakes, or milk, coconut is the darling of grain-free baking. You typically see this fruit very well represented in grain-free cookbooks.

While coconut flour can be a bit tricky to learn to bake with, it has many advantages that are worth the trouble. Unlike wheat flour and many other starchy flours, coconut flour is high in protein, high in fiber, and is exceptionally low on the glycemic index. That means you and your kiddos won't suffer from that mid-morning carb-overload crash.

It also ensures that your brain will be kept out of a fog for the morning ahead, as there are no grains weighing you down and messing up your gut—just pure, grain-free, coconutty goodness.

Much like eggs, coconut oil was vilified for many years due to its high saturated fat content. But coconut oil, in recent years, has risen to the top of the list of the healthiest real-food fats to include in your diet.

Coconut oil is composed of medium-chain triglycerides, which are small, easy to break down molecules. This is important because they are a stellar source of backup energy. Your brain is an energy hog. At just three pounds, it uses 20% of your daily energy input. Your brain's main fuel is glucose. However, it cannot store glucose and without a constant supply of energy, brain cells soon start to die.

Your liver can break down stored fat to produce ketones that can be used as a substitute fuel during times of brain cell starvation. The medium-chain triglycerides in coconut oil can also be broken down into ketones by the liver, and readily cross the blood-brain barrier to provide instant energy to brain cells.

Almond Flour

Almond flour is another alternative flour you'll see used frequently in grain-free cookbooks. It is, quite simply, ground almonds. These nuts include all the macronutrients: protein, healthy fats, and carbohydrates.

Micronutrients like vitamin E, iron, calcium, and potassium are all included in ground blanched almond flour. According to Karen Curley, nutritionist and author at SFGate/Healthy Eating,

> *One ounce of almonds ground into flour adds 6.8 milligrams of vitamin E to your daily vitamin intake. Vitamin E is an antioxidant that helps prevent cell damage, heart disease and stroke. Almond flour also gives you 0.8 milligrams of iron, 65.2 milligrams of magnesium and 57.4 milligrams of calcium in a ¼-cup serving. Calcium helps strengthen your bones and teeth, and helps your circulatory system carry enzymes and hormones throughout your body. Another mineral in almond flour is potassium, which helps regulate blood pressure—¼ cup of almond flour adds 160.4 milligrams of potassium to your diet.*

In simple terms, those small nuts pack a powerfully healthy punch!

Spinach

Fresh spinach is packed with nutrients like folate, vitamin E, and vitamin K. These nutrients can help prevent brain problems like dementia.

In fact, a 2006 *Neurology* study showed that "eating three servings of leafy green, yellow, and cruciferous vegetables a day can delay cognitive decline by 40%."

Getting that many leafy greens into a child's body during the day isn't easy! That's why it's a great idea to start first thing in the morning. Hide them in egg dishes or smoothies if your kids aren't big fans.

Walnuts

Do you know how awesome walnuts are for your brain? I mean, they look like a brain so that should be enough evidence right? Better than their looks, science has uncovered that as little as ¼ cup of walnuts per day can give you almost 100% of the RDA for omega-3 fatty acids.

Foods that are rich in omega-3s should top your brain-friendly food list. Omega-3s assist in optimizing brain function—from depression, cognition, and memory to mental health. In fact, omega-3 fatty acids have actually been shown to increase brain volume.

Eggs

Spinach and Goat Cheese Egg Muffins

Lynnae McCoy

Ingredients

- 12 eggs
- 2 Tablespoons cream (or use milk)
- ½ teaspoon salt
- ¼ teaspoon pepper
- 2 cups fresh baby spinach, packed down a little
- ½ cup goat cheese

Instructions

1. Preheat oven to 350 degrees. Grease a 12-cup muffin tin.

2. In a large bowl, whisk eggs with cream or milk. Add salt and pepper and mix well. Gently stir in spinach.

3. Crumble goat cheese into egg mixture. Mix gently until cheese is mixed in well.

4. Fill each muffin cup in the tin with ⅓ cup egg mixture.

5. Bake egg muffins for 20-25 minutes until a toothpick inserted into the center comes out clean.

6. Let rest in pan 10 minutes before removing, if you don't want the muffins to fall.

To freeze: Lightly grease a cookie sheet. Place egg muffins on top of cookie sheet and freeze until muffins are solid. Store frozen muffins in a labeled Ziploc bag in the freezer. In the morning, just pull out as many as you need, and keep the rest in the freezer.

Fiesta Egg Scramble

Jessica Young

Ingredients

- 4 eggs, beaten until smooth
- 1 pepper, chopped
- ½ onion, chopped
- 1 clove garlic, chopped
- ¼ cup shredded cheese (omit for dairy-free or Paleo)
- a few Tablespoons of healthy cooking fat

Instructions

1. In a fry pan, add the fat and chopped veggies; saute until soft.
2. Pour the beaten eggs over the veggies and stir.
3. Add in the cheese and mix.
4. Cook, while stirring, until the eggs are cooked and no liquid remains.
5. Serve with salsa, hot sauce, and/or guacamole.

PALEO

Leftover Roast Chicken and Leek Frittata

Chantelle Marie Swayne

Ingredients

- 1 cup leftover roast chicken, shredded
- 2 Tablespoons fat from roast chicken
- 1 cup thinly sliced leek
- 5 eggs
- 3 sprigs thyme
- 3 sprigs marjoram
- salt
- pepper

Instructions

1. Place the chicken, fat, and leeks in a fry pan and sauté until the leeks are soft.
2. In a mixing bowl, mix together eggs, herbs, salt, and pepper.
3. Pour egg mixture over chicken and leeks; cover.
4. Cook, covered, on low heat until the eggs are cooked all the way through.
5. Serve with ½ avocado, a side salad, and/or sautéed vegetables for a hearty meal.

This recipe is a great way to use up any leftover roast chicken from the night before and has excellent flavor.

Serve with ½ an avocado for an extra brain boost and a hearty meal that will keep you going until the next time you can fill your belly!

PALEO

Savory Salmon Frittatas

Amanda Espinoza

Ingredients

- 1 cup red bell pepper, diced
- 1 cup broccoli florets, cut small
- 1 small onion, diced (up to 1 cup)
- 2 Tablespoons butter
- 2 Tablespoons olive oil
- 6 eggs
- ⅓ cup sour cream or creme fraiche
- ¼-⅓ cup sharp cheddar cheese, shredded
- 5-7 ounces canned salmon
- salt and pepper to taste

Instructions

1. In a cast iron skillet on med-high heat melt 1 Tablespoon butter and 1 Tablespoon olive oil.
2. Saute diced veggies in butter and oil until broccoli is bright green. Remove when finished.
3. In a separate bowl, beat eggs and cream. Flake salmon into egg mixture and mix well.
4. Add veggies to egg mixture, stirring well.
5. Season with a little salt and pepper, about ¼ teaspoon each.
6. Add 1 Tablespoon butter and 1 Tablespoon olive oil to skillet, melt, then add egg mixture.
7. Cook on medium heat for about 5 minutes or until light brown on the bottom.
8. Sprinkle cheese evenly over the top and place under the broiler till bubbly and brown.

Secret Ingredient Scrambled Eggs

Raia Todd

Ingredients

- 10 eggs
- 2 carrots
- 1 clove garlic
- ¼ cup sour cream or plain yogurt
- 1 teaspoon salt
- dash pepper
- 1 teaspoon parsley
- ½ teaspoon oregano
- ½ teaspoon basil
- ½-1 cup cheddar cheese, shredded (optional)

Instructions

1. Preheat greased skillet over medium heat.
2. Roughly chop carrot and place in the blender with the remainder of the veggies.
3. Pulse until small chunks remain.
4. Add eggs and sour cream and puree.
5. Pour into the skillet and add herbs and cheese.
6. Cook until eggs are desired doneness, stirring frequently to prevent burning.

Spinach Scrambled Eggs Over Fresh Tomatoes

Sarah Robinson

Ingredients

- 1 Tablespoon coconut oil
- ½ to 1 cup spinach, chopped
- ¼ small onion, chopped
- ½ teaspoon garlic powder
- 2 eggs
- 2 tomato slices
- shredded cheese (optional)

Instructions

1. Saute spinach and onion together in coconut oil.
2. Sprinkle with garlic powder.
3. Whisk together 2 eggs.
4. Pour over spinach and onions.
5. Scramble eggs as normal.
6. Place 2 slices of tomato on a plate.
7. Put the spinach onion egg mixture on top of the sliced tomatoes.
8. Top with cheese (optional), salt and pepper.

PALEO

Easy Grain-Free Egg Bake

Paula Miller

Ingredients

- 18 eggs
- 1 medium onion, chopped
- 1 green bell pepper, chopped
- 1 cup raw milk
- 1 cup cheddar cheese, shredded
- 1 pound meat of your choice: precooked ham, browned ground beef, or browned sausage

Instructions

1. Preheat oven to 350 degrees.

2. If you're using ham, have it cut into small pieces. If you're using ground beef, brown 1 pound in a medium frying pan over low to medium heat. You can add the homemade sausage seasoning anytime while the hamburger is browning and stir it in well.

3. Combine the eggs, onion, green pepper, milk, and cheese in large mixing bowl. Whisk together well.

4. Stir in the meat of your choice. Pour into a greased 9x13 pan.

5. Bake for 1 hour until just lightly browned on top.

When shopping for your meat, it's important to look for quality meat—meat that has been grass-fed and allowed to pasture. Animals allowed to pasture are healthier, richer in important fatty acids, and a better source of vitamins and minerals. They also have much less chance of being infected with e. coli and other pathogens.

Hashbrown Cups with Egg & Kale Scramble

Renee Kohley

Ingredients

- 1 large russet potato, shredded (about 2 cups)
- 5 pastured eggs (you may need 6 if your eggs are smaller)
- ¾ cup chopped kale
- ½ teaspoon garlic powder
- ½ teaspoon onion powder
- ½ teaspoon sea salt
- ¼ teaspoon pepper
- sea salt/pepper to taste

Instructions

1. Butter a 6-cup muffin tin, and cover the bottom and sides with the shredded potatoes, forming a "nest."

2. Sprinkle garlic powder, onion powder, sea salt, and pepper over the potatoes, and bake the hashbrown nests at 425 degrees for 15 minutes.

3. Turn the oven down to 350 degrees.

4. Whisk the eggs and kale in a small bowl, and pour the egg mixture into the baked hashbrown nests.

5. Sprinkle salt and pepper on the top and bake at 350 degrees for 20-25 minutes. You can cool and wrap these to freeze! You can also double this into a full 12-cup muffin pan and freeze the leftovers!

PALEO

"Cereals"

Apple Cereal

Sammi Ricke

Ingredients

- 1 apple
- 1 cup plain unsweetened almond milk
- 1 teaspoon vanilla
- 3 drops liquid stevia
- 1 teaspoon hemp seeds
- 1 teaspoon cacao nibs
- 1 Tablespoon ground flax seed
- 1 Tablespoon sliced almonds

Instructions

1. Chop the apple into bite-sized pieces and place in a cereal bowl.

2. Mix the unsweetened almond milk, vanilla, and liquid Stevia in a small dish or mug. Then pour over apples.

3. Top the apple and milk mixture with the remaining ingredients. Enjoy!

PALEO

Grain-Free Banana "Oatmeal"

Becky Marie

Ingredients

- 6 eggs
- 2 bananas (very ripe is best)
- ½ to 1 teaspoon vanilla
- 1 to 2 Tablespoons coconut oil
- Nuts to garnish (optional)

Instructions

1. Mash the bananas with a fork in a bowl.
2. Add eggs and vanilla and beat together until well mixed.
3. Heat coconut oil over medium heat.
4. Add egg mixture and cook like scrambled eggs.

Cranberry Walnut Granola Cereal

Renee Kohley

Ingredients

- 1 pound raw walnuts (about 4 cups)
- 1 pound raw Brazil nuts (about 3 cups)
- 1 pound raw sunflower seeds (about 4 cups)
- 3 Tablespoons sea salt for soaking
- 3 cups unsweetened coconut shreds
- 1 cup avocado oil (melted butter or coconut oil works too)
- ¾ cup - 1 cup pure maple syrup (raw honey works too)
- 1 Tablespoon almond extract
- 2-3 cups dried cranberries

Instructions

1. Put the walnuts, Brazil nuts, sunflower seeds, and salt in a large mixing bowl, add water to cover, and combine well. Set the bowl in a warm spot in your kitchen for 8 hours (I put everything in first thing in the morning, then after dinner get it all in the dehydrator to run overnight).

2. After the nuts/seeds soak, put them in a strainer to drain excess water. It doesn't have to be perfect. Just get what you can off.

3. Meanwhile, put the rest of the ingredients in the large mixing bowl, add the strained nuts/seeds, and combine.

4. Spread out on your dehydrator trays and dry overnight, about 12 hours, at 125-135º F. Break up the dried granola and store in airtight containers.

PALEO

Grain-Free Apple Cinnamon Granola

Renee Kohley

Ingredients

- 3 cups raw sunflower seeds, finely chopped
- 3 cups raw Brazil nuts, finely chopped
- 3 cups raw pecans, finely chopped
- 2 Tablespoons sea salt
- 4 cups unsweetened coconut shreds
- 2 cups coconut flour
- 1 quart applesauce
- 2 Tablespoons almond or vanilla extract
- 1-2 Tablespoons ground cinnamon to taste
- ½ - ¾ cup raw honey
- 1 cup avocado oil, melted butter, or coconut oil
- 5 small/medium apples, chopped

Instructions

1. Soak your nuts/seeds. You can soak them overnight and then dehydrate your granola all day the next day. Or you can soak them all day, and then get the granola into the dehydrator overnight. Put the chopped raw nuts/seeds and the sea salt into a large mixing bowl and add water to the bowl until it covers the nuts/seeds by a good inch. Set the bowl in a warm area of your kitchen for 8-12 hours to soak.

2. After the nuts/seeds have soaked, put them into a strainer to drain.

3. Using a very large bowl or container, add the drained nuts/seeds to the rest of the ingredients.

4. Spread the granola mixture out onto your dehydrator trays and dehydrate at 105-110 degrees about 8 or so hours. If you don't have a dehydrator, you can spread the granola mixture out onto baking sheets and bake at your oven's lowest temperature until it is dried out. You will need to stir the granola around every half hour but it does work just as good and I did it this way for years!

PALEO

Good Morning Trail Mix Muesli

Amanda Espinoza

Ingredients

- 1 cup unsweetened dried shredded coconut
- 1 cup hulled raw pumpkin seeds
- 1 cup whole almonds (soaked and dehydrated are best)
- ½ cup hulled raw sunflower seeds
- ½ cup walnuts (soaked and dehydrated are best)
- stevia to taste (or other sweetener)
- strawberries (optional)

Instructions

1. In a medium-sized mixing bowl, mix coconut flakes, pumpkin seeds, and sunflower seeds.
2. Chop the almonds and walnuts; add to the bowl.
3. Mix all well.
4. Measure out ⅓ cup of the mix into your individual serving dishes.
5. Add 3 sliced or diced strawberries to each bowl.
6. Add your choice of milk, kefir, or yogurt; stir to mix well. I prefer almond or coconut milk.
7. Add stevia or other sweetener to taste; mix again and serve.

You will receive 10 grams of protein from just one serving of the muesli alone, but if you are looking to beef up your protein, consider serving with milk, yogurt, or kefir! This will be a protein-packed meal to get you off to a good start.

P A L E O

Cashew, Fig, and Vanilla Toasted Coconut Granola

Chantelle Marie Swayne

Ingredients

- 1 cup roasted cashews
- ½ cup coconut flakes
- ¼ cup sunflower seeds
- 2 Tablespoons ground flaxseed
- 1 teaspoon cinnamon
- contents of 2 vanilla bean pods, scraped
- pinch of salt
- 2 Tablespoons coconut oil, melted
- 1 Tablespoon maple syrup (optional)
- 6 dried figs, finely chopped

Instructions

1. Mix first 7 ingredients together.
2. Drizzle coconut oil and maple syrup and stir through.
3. Toast on a coconut oil-greased tray for 10 minutes at 350 degrees, stirring the mix around once or twice during cooking to toast evenly
4. Add in figs.
5. Store in a jar in the refrigerator for up to 2 weeks.
6. Serve with almond or coconut milk, or on top of yogurt.

P
A
L
E
O

Apple Butter N'Oatmeal

Sammi Ricke

Ingredients

- 1 cup apple butter
- 1 cup cooked quinoa
- ½ cup coconut flour
- ½ cup ground flax seed
- ¼ cup honey
- 4 eggs
- 1 Tablespoon chia seeds
- 2 teaspoons vanilla
- 1 teaspoon cinnamon
- 1 teaspoon baking soda
- 2 teaspoons baking powder
- ⅛ teaspoon sea salt

Instructions

1. Preheat oven to 400 degrees.
2. Mix all ingredients in medium-sized bowl.
3. Pour batter into a greased 8x8 glass pan, ramekins, or 2 medium-sized bread pans.
4. Bake about 25-30 min or until top is browned and slightly puffed.

Bake times may vary depending on which pan you use. I have made this recipe in each of the pans listed and it has always turned out delicious!

This n'oatmeal is delicious on its own, but I enjoy it with a splash of warm milk and topped with diced apples!

PALEO

Baked Goods

Cheesy Sausage Breakfast Biscuits

Trisha Gilkerson

Ingredients

- 6 eggs
- 6 Tablespoons butter, melted
- ½ teaspoon salt
- ½ teaspoon baking powder
- 1 teaspoon garlic powder
- ½ cup coconut flour
- 8 ounces sharp cheddar cheese
- 1 pound cooked ground

Instructions

1. Preheat oven to 400 degrees and grease 32 mini-muffin tins.
2. Combine the coconut flour, garlic powder, baking powder, and salt.
3. Add the eggs and melted butter. Mix thoroughly.
4. Fold in the cheddar cheese and ground sausage.
5. Fill the mini-muffin tins to the top. Bake at 400 degrees for 12-14 minutes.

BREAKFAST CASSEROLE VARIATION: Instead of baking in mini- muffin tins, bake in a greased 9-inch pie pan. Bake at 400 degrees for 30-35 minutes. This makes a great Saturday morning family breakfast!

Cream Cheese Muffins with Blueberry Syrup

Lynnae McCoy

Ingredients

Muffins

- Muffins
- 2 8-ounce packages cream cheese (not low fat), room temperature
- ¼ cup stevia/erythritol blend (like Truvia or Pyure)
- 2 eggs
- ½ teaspoon vanilla

Topping

- 2 cups blueberries (can be frozen - no need to thaw)
- ¼ cup water
- ½ Tablespoon stevia/erythritol blend sweetener
- ⅛ teaspoon Xanthan Gum (or thickener of your choice)

Instructions

1. Preheat oven to 350 degrees. Liberally grease a muffin pan.

2. Mix together cream cheese, sweetener, eggs, and vanilla until well-blended and smooth.

3. Fill muffin cups with cream cheese mixture, ⅔ full.

4. Bake in preheated oven 18 minutes.

5. Turn heat off and crack oven open and cool in oven for an hour. If you're in a hurry, you can pull them out of the oven right away, but the centers will sink.

6. To make blueberry syrup, heat blueberries, water, and sweetener in covered saucepan over medium heat. When blueberries are soft and warm, stir in xanthan gum. Heat a couple minutes more until syrup slightly thickens.

7. Serve warm or refrigerate until the next morning. My kids prefer them cold. Top with blueberry syrup right before serving.

Honey Walnut Apple Crisp

Raia Todd

Ingredients

- 6-8 cups chopped apples (I like Gala, but any kind would work)
- 2 ½ teaspoons cinnamon
- ¼ teaspoon ginger
- ⅛ teaspoon nutmeg
- ⅛ teaspoon cloves
- ¼ teaspoon kosher salt
- ½ cup honey, divided
- ¼ cup coconut oil, in solid state
- 1 cup finely chopped walnuts

Instructions

1. Preheat oven to 400.
2. Place chopped apples in 9x13 inch baking dish.
3. In small bowl, whisk together spices and salt. Sprinkle over apples and stir to evenly coat.
4. Drizzle with ¼ cup of the honey and stir to evenly coat apples.
5. In same small bowl, cut coconut oil in to walnuts until no chunks of oil remain. Stir in honey, then sprinkle mixture over apples, breaking it up with your hands as you go.
6. Bake for 30-35 minutes, or until apples are tender.

P
A
L
E
O

An easy, grain-free version of an all-time breakfast favorite. Instead of getting the tasty crunch from oats, this apple crisp uses antioxidant-rich walnuts, which can help combat free radical damage to our brains.

Super Food Breakfast Bars

Amanda Espinoza

Ingredients

- 1 cup almond meal
- ¼ cup coconut flour
- ½ teaspoon sea salt
- 1 cup unsweetened shredded coconut flakes
- 1 cup pumpkin seeds
- 1 cup sunflower seeds
- ½ cup chopped or slivered almonds
- ½ cup coconut oil, melted
- 2 teaspoons vanilla
- 40 drops or ½ teaspoon NOW brand organic liquid stevia or other sweetener to taste
- 3 eggs

Instructions

1. Pre-heat oven to 350 degrees.
2. Grease a 9 x 13 inch baking dish with a little coconut oil.
3. Melt the ½ cup coconut oil on low heat.
4. Meanwhile, mix all dry ingredients very well in a large bowl.
5. Add coconut oil, vanilla, stevia, and eggs.
6. Mix VERY well again.
7. Place in the baking dish and pat the mixture evenly into the corners and all through.
8. Bake in oven for about 25 minutes or until browned on the edges and lightly browned on top.

P
A
L
E
O

For extra protein, add a scoop of protein powder. You may need to adjust the liquid, but not by much. I also like to break up my bars and add it on top of Greek yogurt with some berries.

Almond Lemon Biscotti

Lynnae McCoy

Ingredients

- ¼ cup butter, melted and cooled
- 1 egg
- ¼ cup Truvia or other stevia/erythritol blend
- ½ teaspoon almond extract
- ½ teaspoon lemon extract
- zest of one lemon
- 1 ¾ cups almond flour
- ¼ cup protein powder (unflavored)
- ½ teaspoon baking powder
- ½ teaspoon xanthan gum
- ¼ teaspoon salt

Instructions

1. Preheat oven to 375 degrees. Cover a baking sheet with parchment paper.

2. Whisk together melted butter, egg, Truvia, almond extract, lemon extract, and lemon zest in a large bowl.

3. Combine almond flour, protein powder, baking powder, xanthan gum, and salt in a medium bowl.

4. Add almond flour mixture to butter mixture and stir with a wooden spoon until combined.

5. Place dough on parchment lined baking sheet and shape into a flat log (about 8" x 4").

6. Bake at 375 degrees for 20 minutes until slightly brown.

7. Remove biscotti log from oven and turn the oven down to 275. Let biscotti log cool for 15 minutes. Cut the log into uniformly sized pieces (about ½-¾ inch wide). Place cut side down on parchment lined cookie sheet. Bake at 275 for 15 minutes until top side is crisp.

8. Turn biscotti over and bake with the other side up for 15 minutes. Cool completely before enjoying with a piping hot cup of coffee.

Lemon Blueberry Muffins

Lynnae McCoy

Ingredients

- 2 cups almond flour
- ½ cup unflavored protein powder
- ¼ cup Truvia or other stevia/erythritol blend
- ¾ teaspoon baking powder
- ½ cup melted butter
- 1 cup plain, full-fat Greek yogurt
- juice of one lemon
- zest of one lemon
- 1 teaspoon lemon extract
- 2 eggs
- 1 cup frozen blueberries

Instructions

1. Preheat oven to 350 degrees and liberally grease muffin tin.

2. Combine almond flour, protein powder, Truvia, and baking powder, mixing well and making sure all the clumps of almond flour are broken down.

3. In a separate bowl, mix together melted butter, Greek yogurt, lemon juice, lemon zest, and lemon extract. Beat in eggs one at a time.

4. Add wet mixture to dry mixture, stirring until combined. Gently stir in frozen blueberries.

5. Spoon batter into muffin cups. Don't be afraid to fill them all the way up. Almond flour doesn't expand like wheat flour. Bake at 350 degrees for 25-30 minutes.

This grain-free version of a lemon-blueberry muffin is so light you would never guess it's made with almond flour! Greek yogurt provides plenty of moisture. It also provides Tyrosine, which improves mental alertness.

Cinnamon Coconut Breakfast Muffins

Paula Miller

Ingredients (candida-friendly)

- 6 eggs
- ¼ cup milk (coconut milk for paleo or candida-friendly)
- ¼ cup coconut oil
- ¼ cup honey (or 3 Tablespoons xylitol for candida-friendly)
- ½ teaspoon sea salt
- 1 teaspoon vanilla
- ½ cup coconut flour
- ½ teaspoon baking powder
- 1 teaspoon cinnamon
- 1 teaspoon nutmeg
- ½ cup unsweetened coconut flakes
- ⅔ cup nuts (almonds, walnuts, etc.)

Instructions

1. If making original version, preheat oven to 400 degrees. For the candida-friendly version using coconut milk and xylitol, preheat to 375 degrees.
2. Grease muffin pan with coconut oil.
3. Combine coconut oil, milk, xylitol or honey, salt, and vanilla.
4. Add the coconut flour, baking powder, cinnamon, nutmeg, coconut flakes, and nuts. If your eggs and milk are cold, your coconut oil may begin to harden. Simply break the coconut oil chunks apart with a fork and the rest will melt and bake into the muffins.
5. Fill 6 muffin cups into nice, heaping mounds.
6. Bake 15-20 minutes. Let cool about 10 minutes before removing.

Makes 6 muffins

Waffles, Donuts, and Pancakes

Apple Cinnamon Walnut Crepes

Amanda Espinoza

Crepes | Ingredients

- 10 eggs
- ⅓ cup cream or coconut milk
- 1 teaspoon cinnamon
- dash of vanilla
- pinch of sea salt

Instructions

1. In a large bowl beat eggs, cream, vanilla, & salt.
2. Pre-heat skillet to med-high heat and melt coconut oil or butter
3. Add about ⅓ cup egg mixture to pan and roll pan around to spread the egg mixture thin.
4. Look for when edges roll up. Just as the bottom gets done, flip gently to cook both sides evenly. Just about 30 seconds or so and the crepe will be done.
5. Between every 3-4 crepes you will need to re-grease the skillet, so keep the oil or butter handy. *Note* You might also need to reduce the heat as you cook. I start at med-high and end up reducing to low as things cook.
6. Stack cooked crepes on plate covered with a clean cloth and keep warm in the oven.

Filling | Ingredients

- 2 large granny smith apples, diced large
- 1-1 ½ cups chopped walnuts
- 2 Tablespoons butter
- 1 teaspoon cinnamon
- ½ teaspoon vanilla
- pinch of salt
- sweetener to taste, if desired

Instructions

1. Clean skillet out and melt butter on medium-high heat.
2. Saute diced apples.
3. Stir in cinnamon, vanilla, salt, and sweetener.
4. Add walnuts and heat through.

Putting it together:

1. Lay a crepe on a plate.
2. Add up to ½ cup filling per crepe.
3. Roll or fold crepe.

Carrot Cake "Fritter" Pancakes

Jennifer Saleem

Ingredients

- 2 large eggs
- 3 Tablespoons coconut oil
- ¾ cup coconut milk
- ¼ cup raw honey or maple syrup
- 1 ½ cups cassava flour
- 2 teaspoons baking soda
- 1 ½ teaspoons vanilla bean powder
- 1 teaspoon cinnamon
- ⅛ teaspoon nutmeg (use more if you like a little more spiciness)
- ⅛ teaspoon cloves (use more if you like a little more spiciness)
- ¼ teaspoon ginger
- 2 cups grated carrot (you want to get this really finely grated, almost pulp-like)

These pancakes freeze well. Double or triple the batch, cool, freeze, then reheat from frozen in a toaster oven for about 15 minutes at 350 degrees.

Instructions

1. Combine the eggs, coconut oil, and milk in a large bowl and beat together.
2. Add the honey or maple syrup and beat some more.
3. Add the rest of the ingredients, one by one, with the exception of the carrots. Mix together until everything is well blended.
4. Slowly fold in the carrots.
5. Heat a large skillet over medium heat.
6. Coat with coconut oil.
7. Spoon about ¼ cup of the batter onto the griddle, making little mounds. Flatten a tad with a spatula.
8. Cook for about two minutes or until the tops are covered in bubbles and the edges start to brown.
9. Flip the pancake and cook another 2 minutes or so.
10. Repeat until all the batter is used up.
11. Serve warm.

Banana Walnut Mini Donuts with Dark Chocolate Glaze

Raia Todd

Donuts | Ingredients

- 2 bananas (about 1 cup mashed)
- 1 ½ cups walnut pieces
- 2 eggs
- 1 teaspoon vanilla
- 2 Tablespoons honey
- 6 Tablespoons tapioca starch
- ½ teaspoon baking soda

Makes about 4 dozen mini donuts.

Instructions

1. Preheat oven to 325 degrees and grease mini donut pan(s).
2. Place bananas, walnuts, eggs, vanilla, and honey in a blender. Puree until smooth, then add starch and soda. Pulse to combine.
3. Pour slowly into greased mini donut pans, filling rings about ½ full (about 1 tablespoon).
4. Bake at 325 degrees for 15 minutes.
5. Cool in pans for 5 minutes, then remove with a spoon and cool before glazing.

Dark Chocolate Glaze | Ingredients

- 2 Tablespoons honey
- 2 Tablespoons coconut oil
- 3 Tablespoons cocoa powder
- splash of vanilla
- pinch of sea salt
- 2 Tablespoons coarsely ground walnuts for topping

Instructions

1. Combine all ingredients in a small bowl, except for walnuts - place them in a separate bowl.
2. Dip cooled donuts in glaze and then dip in chopped walnuts.

Sweet Potato Pancakes

Chantelle Marie Swayne

Ingredients

- 1 cup sweet potato (any variety), skin removed, cooked, cooled, and pureed (You won't taste this! I use leftovers from another night.)
- ¼ cup coconut flour
- 4 eggs
- 4 Tablespoons coconut milk
- 1 teaspoon baking soda
- 1 teaspoon cinnamon
- ¼ teaspoon vanilla
- 4 teaspoons coconut oil

Instructions

1. In a food processor or high-speed blender, blend the sweet potato until smooth, then add the rest of the ingredients and blend until smooth.

2. Heat a fry pan on low-medium with 1 teaspoon coconut oil.

3. Pour ¼ of the mixture into the pan, and gently spread around into a circle shape.

4. Sear the pancake for 5 seconds, then turn the heat down to low (for my stovetop, this was the very lowest setting). Cook for a further 1 ½ - 2 minutes before flipping gently.

5. Keep the heat on low and cook for an additional 1 - 1 ½ minutes.

6. Repeat steps 3-5 with the remaining mixture.

From a nutritional stand point, a fantastic flour to use in gluten-free cooking is coconut flour. Unlike many other gluten-free flours, coconut flour is low on the glycemic index and won't cause blood sugar spikes. Coconut flour is also high in protein, fiber, maganese, and lauric acid (a saturated fat that is essential for your immune function).

Easy Peasy Gluten-Free Crepes

Kelli Becton

Ingredients

- 1 cup cold water
- 2 eggs
- 2 Tablespoons melted butter (or coconut oil for Paleo version)
- 3 Tablespoons sugar
- 1 ½ cup grain-free pancake mix (or a mix of your favorite grain-free flours)

Instructions

1. Mix ingredients and let stand at room temperature to thicken - about 12 minutes.

2. In a HOT skillet, add a pat of butter or non-stick spray and then pour just enough batter into the pan to cover the bottom of the pan. You can adjust thickness of crepes according to how you like them best.

3. Once bubbles form and stay, use spatula to flip. The second side won't take as long, so be quick!

4. Remove crepe from skillet and continue until all batter is gone. You can store them in the fridge for about a week, or wrap well and freeze.

These crepes are easy peasy and delicious, especially for the mom who's on the go!

Maple Bacon Waffles

Jennifer Saleem

The Bacon | Ingredients

- 1 pound nitrate-free bacon slices (pork and beef bacon work better than turkey bacon)
- ¼ cup maple syrup

Instructions

1. Preheat oven to 400 degrees.
2. Place the bacon slices on a large baking sheet lined with parchment paper and bake for 10 minutes.
3. Brush the bacon slices with maple syrup and pour off the excess fat from the pan.
4. Continue baking until the bacon is crispy, about 5-10 minutes more
5. Allow to cool for a few minutes, then crumble into smallish pieces.

Top these waffles with cinnamon apple topping (see page 73 for recipe).

The Waffles | Ingredients

- 12 eggs
- 1 Tablespoon vanilla bean paste or 2 teaspoons vanilla extract
- ¾ cup butter or coconut oil, melted
- ¾ cup coconut flour, sifted
- 1 teaspoon baking soda
- ⅓ cup milk of choice
- dash of sea salt
- the crumbled maple bacon pieces

Instructions

1. Mix the eggs and vanilla on low until the eggs are just slightly frothy.
2. Add the melted butter/oil and mix on low for about 20 seconds.
3. Add the coconut flour and baking soda and mix on medium until everything is incorporated.
4. Add ⅓ cup milk and salt (if using) and mix for 30 seconds.
5. Allow batter to sit for two minutes. After two minutes, check the consistency. It should be thick but still able to drip off a spoon. If it is too thick, add a splash of milk and mix again. Continue until you have the right consistency that you know works in your waffle maker.
6. Add the bacon pieces and fold in slowly.
7. Follow your waffle iron's instructions from that point forward.

Cinnamon Apple Topping

CINNAMON APPLES OPTION 1 | JENNIFER SALEEM

Ingredients

- 2 sweeter apples, peeled and sliced
- 1 teaspoon ground cinnamon
- ¼ teaspoon ground nutmeg
- 2 Tablespoons water
- ¼ cup butter, ghee, or coconut oil, melted

Instructions

1. Place the apple slices in a bowl with the water, cinnamon, and nutmeg.
2. Toss the apples to cover in spices.
3. Place the apple mixture in an oven safe bowl and drizzle with the butter/oil. Cover loosely with foil or parchment paper.
4. Cook in your 400 degree oven for about 10 minutes. Check to see if the apples are still moist. You may need to add more water or butter. You do not want them drying out.
5. Continue baking until the apples are tender. This usually takes a total of 20 minutes for me since I slice the apples really thin.

CINNAMON APPLES OPTION 2 | KELLI BECTON

Ingredients

- 5-6 large crisp apples (peeled, cored, and chopped into bite-sized chunks)
- 1 cup brown sugar
- 3 teaspoons ground cinnamon or
- ¼ teaspoon ground nutmeg
- ¼ teaspoon ground cloves
- ¼ teaspoon ginger
- 2 Tablespoons of lemon juice
- pinch of salt

Instructions

1. Mix apples and ingredients thoroughly in large bowl.
2. Cook on medium high heat in large pot, covered, until soft.
3. Stir regularly; you may add a pat of butter if needed.
4. Serve over warm pancakes.

Gluten-Free Pancakes

Kelli Becton

Ingredients

- 3 large eggs
- 1 Tablespoon water
- 1 Tablespoon vanilla
- 2 Tablespoons honey
- 1 ½ cups blanched almond flour
- A pinch of salt
- ¼ teaspoon baking soda
- oil in pan for cooking (coconut oil or butter)

Instructions

1. With a fork, blend eggs, water, vanilla, and honey.
2. Mix in almond flour, pinch of salt, and baking soda until well-combined.
3. Heat oil in large skillet over medium heat.
4. Use a spoon to scoop a heaping tablespoon of batter into the skillet.
5. When pancakes show little bubbles all around, flip pancakes over and cook other side and remove.
6. Repeat process with remaining batter.

Top these waffles with cinnamon apple topping (see page 73 for recipe).

Smoothies

Mint Chocolate Chip Breakfast Smoothie

Sammi Ricke

Ingredients

- 1 cup plain Greek yogurt
- 2 teaspoons raw local honey
- 2 cups spinach
- 2 frozen bananas, sliced
- ½ cup unsweetened almond milk
- 3 Tablespoons chocolate chips (I use Enjoy Life minis)
- 2 Tablespoons ground flaxseed
- 2 teaspoons hemp seeds or 1 teaspoon chia seeds
- ¼ -½ teaspoon mint extract

Instructions

1. Combine honey and yogurt in a small bowl then put in the blender.
2. Top with the remaining ingredients and blend until smooth.

Coco-Cado Lime Smoothie

Amanda Espinoza

Ingredients

- 1 avocado, seeded
- 1 cucumber, peeled and roughly chopped
- 1 stalk celery, roughly chopped
- 2-4 cups spinach
- 1-2 limes (depends on your taste)
- 1 can full-fat coconut milk (or a little less than 2 cups full-fat kefir)
- 1 teaspoon vanilla (optional)
- stevia to taste
- 1-2 Tablespoons coconut oil

Instructions

1. First, scoop the avocado into the blender.
2. Add all the other ingredients in and blend until smooth. (I used my Magic Bullet with the blender attachment and it works beautifully!)
3. You may enjoy it as is, refrigerate, or add ice to the mix before you blend. I can never wait and I do not put in the ice. I drink straight away and it is heavenly!

Throw out the highly-processed fats like canola and vegetable oil. Replace them with natural, nourishing fats — coconut oil, avocado, grass-fed butter, and yes, even lard.

Fruity Green Smoothie

Sarah Robinson

Ingredients

- 2 oranges
- 5-10 ounces fresh spinach
- 1 cup of water (or almond milk, for a creamier smoothie)
- 1-2 cups frozen strawberries
- 2 frozen bananas

Instructions

1. Peel oranges and place in blender. Blend them first so you have lots of juice while blending the greens.
2. Fill up the blender with spinach.
3. Add a cup of water or almond milk.
4. Blend until smooth.
5. Add frozen strawberries and bananas.

This will keep in the refrigerator for a couple of days.

PALEO

Nut Butter Banana Smoothie

Raia Todd

Ingredients

- 2 very ripe bananas (you can use unspotted ones, but it won't be as sweet)
- 1 – 1 ½ cups milk of choice
- ⅓ cup nut butter of your choice
- 2 Tablespoons chia meal (optional, or chia seeds)
- 1 teaspoon vanilla
- 16 or so ice cubes

Instructions

1. Place all ingredients in blender.
2. Whirl on high for 2 minutes.

PALEO

Immune Booster Smoothie

Renee Kohley

Ingredients

- ¾ cup frozen organic blueberries (could use any frozen berries)
- 1 cup whole, raw milk, yogurt, or coconut milk for a paleo version
- 1-2 Tablespoons organic coconut oil, melted
- juice of ½ lemon
- 2 Tablespoons cold soluble grass-fed collagen
- 1 Tablespoon homemade elderberry syrup
- vitamin C & probiotics per supplement dosing directions

Instructions

1. Place everything into blender.
2. Blend until smooth.

P A L E O

Chocolate Banana Power Smoothie

Renee Kohley

Ingredients

- 2 frozen bananas
- 1 Tablespoon organic cacao powder
- 1-2 scoops Vital Proteins Gelatin (Cold Soluble)
- 1 capsule Mega SporeBiotic or whatever probiotics you may be using
- 1 - 1½ milk of your choice
- 1-2 Tablespoons fat (coconut oil or raw egg yolks, optional but good for fast oxidizers, or kids with AD/HD patterns)
- ¼ cup cooked or frozen chopped kale
- vanilla stevia drops to taste (optional)
- pinch sea salt
- ½ teaspoon camu camu or other whole food c powder

Instructions

1. Place all ingredients into blender or Vitamix.
2. Blend for 2 minutes on high speed.

5 Ingredient Mixed Berry Smoothie

Trisha Gilkerson

Ingredients

- 1 can coconut milk
- 2 cups frozen mixed berries
- ¼ cup xylitol
- ⅛ teaspoon stevia
- ½ teaspoon vanilla

Instructions

1. Place all ingredients in the blender.
2. Whiz around until well-mixed. Enjoy!

P
A
L
E
O

Looking to add some extra protein to a smoothie? Just add a scoop of hydrolyzed collagen. This unique superfood, is virtually tasteless and can be dissolved in hot or cold liquids. It will give a nice protein boost and impart numerous other health benefits!

Cinnamon & Chocolate Red Maca Smoothie

Paula Miller

Ingredients

- ½ cup almond or coconut milk
- ¼ cup water
- 15 ice cubes
- 1 Tablespoon cacao powder
- 2 teaspoons red maca powder (you can increase this gradually)
- 1 teaspoon vanilla
- ⅛ teaspoon almond extract
- ⅛ teaspoon ground cinnamon
- 1 pinch celtic sea salt
- stevia to taste

Instructions

1. Combine all ingredients in a high-powered blender. Blend until smooth.

2. Pour into tall glass and enjoy.

P
A
L
E
O

Dairy-Free Pumpkin Pie Smoothie

Jessica Young

Ingredients

- ½ cup pumpkin puree
- ⅓ cup coconut milk
- good handful of ice
- 1 teaspoon vanilla
- 3 teaspoons cinnamon
- ⅛ teaspoon cloves
- dash of ginger
- dash of sea salt
- stevia to taste (or maple syrup!)

Instructions

1. Add everything to a high-powered blender.
2. Blend until smooth.

This recipe makes about one pint.

P
A
L
E
O

Other Fun Breakfast Options

Mini Breakfast Pizzas

TJ Sugden

Ingredients

Crust

- 4 eggs
- ¼ cup sour cream
- ¼ cup coconut flour
- ¼ cup cheese, finely shredded (any kind)
- 1 teaspoon garlic salt
- ½ teaspoon dried basil
- ½ teaspoon dried parsley
- ½ teaspoon dried oregano
- ½ teaspoon onion powder
- ¼ teaspoon dill

Toppings

- 2 Tablespoons unsalted butter, melted
- eggs
- toppings of choice
- shredded cheese

Instructions

1. Preheat the oven to 350 degrees. Line a baking sheet with either parchment paper or a silicone baking mat.

2. Whisk the 4 eggs in a medium bowl until thoroughly beaten. Whisk in the remaining crust ingredients. The resulting batter will be pretty runny.

3. Pour the batter into about 4 3-inch round circles on the prepared baking sheet (they may spread a bit once poured). Bake for 15 to 20 minutes or until set. Repeat with the remaining batter.

4. Once the mini crusts are baked, brush with melted butter. Top with your choice of a fried/sunny side up egg or scrambled eggs (remember not to overcook the scrambled eggs or they will weep). Place any toppings of choice over the egg, sprinkle with some cheese, then pop back in the oven for an additional five minutes to lightly melt the cheese and heat the toppings.

Brain Boosting Breakfast Salad

TJ Sugden

Ingredients

- lettuce of choice, torn into bite-sized pieces (I prefer bib and romaine lettuce mixed with some spinach leaves)
- 1 egg
- half an avocado, sliced
- 1 handful soaked and toasted pumpkin seeds
- 2 Tablespoons crumbled goat or feta cheese (omit for Paleo version)
- 4 or 5 grape tomatoes, halved
- 2 slices bacon, cooked and crumbled
- salad dressing of choice (optional)

Instructions

1. Place enough lettuce for one serving in a bowl or on a plate.

2. Cook an egg as desired. I prefer a sunny-side up egg where the yolk is runny as this negates the necessity for salad dressing. However, cook it as you like (over-easy, over-medium, over-hard, hard-boiled, soft-boiled, etc.). Place over the top of the lettuce.

3. Toss in the avocado, cheese, tomatoes, and bacon. Drizzle with salad dressing of choice (or omit as that runny egg yolk really does a pretty tasty job) and serve.

Not many people consider salad a breakfast dish, but the recipe I'm sharing with you isn't just any salad. It's ingredients were carefully selected and united to create a breakfast that's sure to boost your child's brain power and also be tasty!

Baked Fruit and Nut Cups

Jessica Young

Ingredients

- ¼ cup pumpkin seeds
- ¼ cup walnuts
- ¼ cup almonds
- ¼ cup pecans
- ¼ cup chia seeds or ground flax seeds
- 2 Tablespoons erythitol (or sucanat for Paleo)
- ½ teaspoon molasses
- 1 Tablespoon coconut oil
- 1 Tablespoon gelatin
- ½ teaspoon cinnamon
- ⅛ teaspoon salt
- ½ cup blueberries (or 1 cup strawberries)
- ¼ cup water

Instructions

1. Pulse all ingredients in a blender until coarsely ground.
2. Press into muffin liners.
3. Bake at 350 degrees for 40 minutes (longer if you want them crispy).
4. Makes a dozen cups.

Chia Berry Pudding

Trisha Gilkerson

Ingredients

- 1 pound fresh berries
- ¼ teaspoon pure stevia extract (or sweeten to taste with sweetener of choice)
- 1 teaspoon vanilla
- 1 ½ cups full-fat coconut milk
- ½ cup chia seeds

Instructions

1. Place everything except the chia seeds in a food processor and blend until smooth.
2. Pour mixture into glass bowl; stir in chia seeds well.
3. Cover and refrigerate 3+ hours. Serve!

While chia seeds used to be most well known for growing the ever-popular "chia pets" they're quickly gaining notoriety as a health food. These little seeds are packed with protein, fat, fiber, vitamins, and minerals. And they pack a powerful punch of antioxidants! They are one of the best sources of important Omega 3 fatty acids.

Sweet Potato and Greens Breakfast Saute

Renee Kohley

Ingredients

- 4-5 strips of pastured bacon, chopped
- ½ medium onion, chopped
- 2 cloves garlic, minced
- 1 large sweet potato, chopped
- 1 box organic spinach
- sea salt/pepper to taste

Instructions

1. Fry bacon and set aside. LEAVE bacon grease behind in the pan to cook in!
2. Saute onion and sweet potato with a few pinches of sea salt for about 10 minutes.
3. Add garlic and cook for a minute.
4. Add spinach and cooked bacon and cook until spinach wilts.
5. Add seasoning to taste.